AF131140

**Columbia University**

STUDIES IN ROMANCE PHILOLOGY
AND LITERATURE

# DOÑA MARÍA DE ZAYAS Y SOTOMAYOR

# DOÑA MARÍA DE ZAYAS Y SOTOMAYOR

## A CONTRIBUTION TO THE STUDY
## OF HER WORKS

BY

LENA E. V. SYLVANIA

SUBMITTED IN PARTIAL FULFILMENT OF THE REQUIREMENTS FOR THE
DEGREE OF DOCTOR OF PHILOSOPHY, IN THE FACULTY OF
PHILOSOPHY, COLUMBIA UNIVERSITY

NEW YORK
COLUMBIA UNIVERSITY PRESS
1922

PRESS OF
THE NEW ERA PRINTING COMPANY
LANCASTER, PA.

TO
MY PARENTS

## PREFACE

The following study is part of a work now in preparation on the subject of the little-known writings of Doña María de Zayas y Sotomayor. This work contemplates a comparatively exhaustive treatment of the author's short stories, her poetry, her play *Traición en la amistad,* and the relative importance of these in literature. It will be accompanied in its completed form by as detailed a bibliography as possible of the entire field. On a subject as extensive as this, it has not been feasible to compress into these few pages more than the discovered facts of the author's life, her salient ideas as exposed in her works, a sketch of the general framework of her short stories, and a study of two of them in particular—*El jardin engañoso* and *El castigo de la miseria.* That Doña María was an ardent feminist is displayed throughout her stories; and this characteristic trait I have stressed as being especially interesting and significant.

I welcome this opportunity to express my sincere gratitude to Professor de Onís, who first interested me in Doña María de Zayas, for his advice, criticism and assistance in the preparation of this study; to Professor H. A. Todd to whom I feel especially indebted for his never-failing sympathetic encouragement, for his many valuable suggestions in connection with the work and for the painstaking reading and revision of the manuscript; to Professor Raymond Weeks for his friendly interest and helpful ideas throughout my course of study at Columbia; and, lastly, to my friend Miss Elsa G. Rust, whose confidence in my efforts has always been a source of inspiration.

LENA E. V. SYLVANIA

COLUMBIA UNIVERSITY,
April 21, 1922.

# CONTENTS

# DOÑA MARÍA DE ZAYAS Y SOTOMAYOR: A CONTRIBUTION TO THE STUDY OF HER WORKS

## CHAPTER I

### INTRODUCTORY

V ERY little is known of the life of Doña María de Zayas y Sotomayor and the little that has been gleaned through careful and painstaking research in connection with the present study is indeed too meagre to satisfy natural curiosity concerning a woman whose loyal and sturdy advocacy of the rights of her sex took a bold and fearless stand which may be considered unique for the times in which she lived. In her writings she voiced the protest that throughout the succeeding years has grown ever more insistent, in its effort to readjust standards of morals and to assure to women an attitude of fairness and justice on the part of the opposite sex. This protest which, at that time and up to just a few years ago, seemed so bizarre to some and so trivial to others, has, by reason of organized effort, attained such importance that it is one of the factors to be reckoned with in both the public and private life of today. Doña María de Zayas y Sotomayor can well be classed with those who first braved public opinion to assert and maintain, by force of argument, that women have certain rights and that, as human beings, they are not inferior to men.

As the preface to her works proclaims, Doña María de Zayas y Sotomayor was a native of Madrid in Spain. Furthermore, we learn from church records that she was baptized in that city in the parish of San Sebastián, on September 12, 1590.[1] Her father was D. Fernando de Zayas y Sotomayor, born in Madrid and baptized in the same parish, November 9, 1566.[2] He was the son of D.

[1] *Apuntes para una Biblioteca de Escritoras Españolas:* Manuel Serrano y Sanz, Madrid, MCMIII. 2 vols. Vol. ii, p. 584.

[2] *Hijos de Madrid, Ilustres en Santidad, Dignidades, Armas, Ciencias y Artes:* D. Joseph Antonio Alvarez y Baena. Madrid, MDCCLXXXIX. 4 vols. In vol. ii, p. 48, Baena expresses the opinion that, in view of the date at which

Francisco de Zayas, a resident of Madrid, although born in Villa
de los Santos de Maimona (situated near Zafra, in Extremadura),
and his mother was Doña Luisa de Zayas of Madrid. His grandparents on his father's side were Alonso de Zayas, born in Zafra
and a resident of Madrid, and Inés Sanchez of Los Santos. On
his mother's side his grandparents were D. Antonio de Sotomayor
and Doña Catalina de Zayas, both of Madrid. D. Fernando de
Zayas was a military man, holding the position of Captain of
Infantry. In 1628 he was admitted to the Order of Santiago, for
which organization he filled the office of " Corregidor de la en-
comienda" of Jerez from August 5, 1638 to November 5, 1642.[3]
Of his wife, we know almost nothing. We are simply told in the
baptismal record of her daughter that she was Doña María de
Barasa.[4]

It seems probable that Doña María de Zayas y Sotomayor lived
in Madrid during the greater part of her life, if not the whole of it.
The fact that her novels were first published in Zaragoza[5] is not
sufficient reason to conclude that she necessarily lived at any time
in that city, although this seems to have remained a question in the
minds of some authorities on Spanish literature.[6] The place of

the author flourished in her literary work, she was doubtless the daughter of D.
Fernando de Sayas y Sotomayor. His supposition is confirmed by the researches
of Manuel Serrano y Sanz, who discovered the baptismal records. [Wherever
early texts are quoted the intention has been to preserve the original orthog-
raphy, punctuation and use of accents.]

[3] *Apuntes:* Manuel Serrano y Sanz. Vol. ii, p. 584.

[4] The baptismal record as given in the *Apuntes*, vol. ii, p. 585, is as follows:
María de Çayas.—En doce dias del mes de Septiembre de mill y quinientos
y noventa años, yo el bachiller Altamirano, theniente de cura bapticé á María,
hija de don Fernando de Çayas y de doña María de Barasa su muger. Pad-
rinos don Diego de Santoyo y doña Juana de Cardona su muger; testigos
Bernabé Gonzales y Alonso García-Altamirano (Madrid, Parroquía de San
Sebastian. Libro tres de bautismos, folio 213).
Strange to say, in spite of the baptismal record, Manuel Serrano y Sanz
tells us in his comment that *Catalina de Barrasa* was the mother's name.
This is the name given by certain other authorities also.

[5] *Novelas amorosas exemplares,* compuestas por Doña María de Zayas y
Sotomayor; Zaragoza, 1637. *Primera y Segunda Parte de las Novelas Amorosas y Exemplares,* compuestas por Doña María de Zayas y Sotomayor: Zaragoza, 1647.

[6] *Biblioteca de Autores Españoles:* Novelistas posteriores a Cervantes,
Tomo 2, con un bosquejo histórico sobre la novela española, escrito por D.
Eustaquid Fernandez de Navarrete. Madrid 1854. M. Rivadeneyra, Ed.

publication may have been merely a matter of convenience, as will appear from the following considerations. It must be remembered that after the Court was established in a permanent manner at Madrid in 1561, a rapid development along social, economic and intellectual lines characterized the city. One of the manifestations of intellectual development at this time was the increased activity in the writing of books. The establishment of printing in the capital in 1566 stimulated to such an extent the publication of these literary efforts that the presses were unable to cope with the demands made upon them. Moreover, court business, including the publication of documents, records and official correspondence submitted for printing, added to the difficulties and burden of work imposed on the press. The situation, instead of becoming better, grew worse.[9] Authors and booksellers alike clamored in vain for more speed and less delay. It was natural that they should look elsewhere for better service if such were to be had. The formalities connected with the issuance of a book, such as the details of examination, censure, license and special privileges, had to be transacted at Madrid,[10] but there was nothing to prevent its actual publication elsewhere. Accordingly, it was no unusual custom to resort to the presses outside the city of Madrid where the pressure was not so great, and where the work could be accomplished far more expeditiously. It is a fact that the publishers and booksellers in cities such as Zaragoza, Valencia and especially Barcelona worked so quickly that they often reprinted popular books and introduced them into Castile before the first Madrid edition of the same was exhausted.[11] Might this not have been the case with the works of Doña María de Zayas?

[9] *Bibliografía Madrileña:* Cristóbal Pérez Pastor, Madrid 1891, vol. i, p. xvii.

[10] *Bibliografía Madrileña:* C. Pérez Pastor. Madrid 1891. Vol. i, p. xiv. " Por orden de Felipe II de 7 de Septiembre de 1558 se manda en el artículo 3° que no se imprima ningún libro en España sin licencia del Consejo Real." P. xv. Another law, in 1592: " . . . las licencias que se dieren para imprimir de nuevo algunos libros de cualquier condición que sean se den por el Presidente y los del nuestro Consejo, y no en otras partes."

[11] *Bibliografía Madrileña:* C. Pérez Pastor. Vol. i, p. xlii. " Zaragoza parece que logró la buena suerte en aquel tiempo de ser pueblo elegido para la impresion de libros de entretenimiento." Bibl. de Aut. Esp.: Novelistas post. a Cervantes; Preface.

Whether Doña María was married or not, we do not know. There is no discovered document, notice or reference in or out of her works to establish this point.[12]   D. Manuel Serrano y Sanz,[13] who has gleaned, thus far, more information on our author than any other investigator, confesses that he has been unable to unearth anything definite concerning the personal life of the Doña María de Zayas in question.   The greatest difficulty encountered in such an investigation is that during the seventeenth century the name of María de Zayas was a very common one.   In the death notices of ladies bearing this name there is nothing to identify any one of them as the author of the "Novelas."   She was doubtless a lady of the Court, aristocratic to her finger tips, well educated and surrounded with friends of similar station and similar tastes.   The fact that she followed her bent and indulged her taste for publishing what she wrote indicates that she must necessarily have been well endowed with the goods of this world, for then as now the Muses were strangely blind to mundane needs.[14]   The pursuit of happiness in their name is indeed a labor of love.   The poets and other authors of her day held her in high esteem, inserting in their verses and prose writings warm praise of her achievements.   Foremost among these were Lope de Vega and Juan Pérez de Montalván.

In his *Laurel de Apolo* Lope de Vega addresses these verses to Doña María de Zayas:

> O dulces Hipocrénides hermosas,
> Los espinos Pangeos
> Aprisa desnudad, y de las rosas
> Texed ricas guirnaldas y trofeos
> A la inmortal Doña María de Zayas;
> Que sin pasar á Lesbos, ni á las playas

[12] D. Eustaquid Fernández de Navarrete says: " ¿Residía en ella (Zaragosa) Doña María, y había en ella contraído uno de esos dulces lazos que fijan la suerto de las criaturas? Ne se sabe." Cf. *Bibl. de Aut. Esp.:* Novelistas post. a Cervantes.

[13] *Apuntes,* Vol. ii, p. 583.

[14] A Doña María de Zayas y Sotomayor sus apellidos la califican de persona de nacimiento distinguido y de clase acomodada.  Solo de este modo pudo tener espacio y desahoga para dedicarse a las letras, porque en España, entonces como ahora, pocos adeptos de las musas podían vivir de las ofrendas que el público rendía en sus altares." Cf. *Bibl. de Aut. Esp.:* Novelistas Post. a Cervantes.

Del vasto mar Egeo,
Que hoy llora el negro velo de Teseo,
A Sapho gozara Mitilenea,
Quien ver milagros de muger desea:
Porque su ingenio, vivamente claro,
Estan único y raro,
Que ella sola pudiera,
No solo pretender la verde rama,
Pero sola ser sol de tu ribera;
Y tu por ella conseguir mas fama,
Que Nápoles por Claudia, por Cornelia
La sacra Roma, y Tebas por Targelia.

Juan Pérez de Montalván in his turn was unstinting in his tribute which appeared in the form of a sonnet in the preliminary pages of the first part of Doña María's *Novelas:*

Dulce Sirena, que la voz sonora
   Apolo te prestó desde su esfera,
   De la Accidalia diosa, verdadera
   Imagen, por quien Marte tierno llora.

Luz destos valles, que qual blanca Aurora
   Fertilizas su verde Primavera,
   Cuya eloquencia aficionar pudiera
   Al Rubio amante, que un Laurel adora.

Prevengate la fama mil Altares,
   Su guirnalda te dé el senor de Delo,
   Quede tu nombre en bronzes esculpido,

El Laurel merecido
   Te dè, Amarilis, la parlera fama,
   Que ya por fin igual tu lyra llama.

Another friend who lived on intimate terms with her was Doña Ana Caro Mallén de Soto, who was also a poet and deeply interested in the field of letters. *Décimas* by her appear in the above-mentioned edition of the *Novelas* and reveal the high admiration she felt for the intellectual attainments of her brilliant contemporary and friend:

Crezca la Gloria Española,
 insigne doña Maria,
 por ti sola, pues podria
 gloriarse España en ti sola:
 nueva Sapho, nueva Pola
 Argentaria, honor adquieres
 a Madrid, y te prefieres
 con soberanos renombres,
 nuevo prodigio a los hõbres,
 nuevo assõbro a las mugeres.
A inmortal region anhelas
 quãdo el aplauso te aclama,
 y al imperio de tu fama
 en sus mismas alas buelas:
 novedades, y novelas
 tu pluma escrive, tu cantas
  triunfo alegre, dichas tantas,
 pues ya tan gloriosa vives,
 q' admiras con lo q' escrives,
 con lo que cantas encantas.
Tu entender esclarecido,
 gran Sibila Mantuana,
 te miente al velo de humana,
 emula al comun olvido;
 y del tiempo desmentido
 lo caduco, a las historias,
 harà eternas tus memorias,
 rindiendole siempre fieles,
 a tu eloquencia, laureles,
 a tu erudicion, vitorias.

# CHAPTER II

## Feminism in the Works of Doña María

Doña María was a woman of advanced ideas, advocating general education for women, recognition of the equal rights of both sexes, and respect for women in the eyes of men. To understand her point of view, to comprehend how noble were her aims and how justified her protest against the position of women in Spain at the time, it is necessary to have a correct perspective of the age, especially as regards woman. Not until this view has been attained can we judge how well or how inadequately she succeeded in portraying, through her works, the manners and customs, the tendencies, and the abuses of the period. As a general thing education for women, however elevated their station might be, was rare. No opportunity was offered for any but a domestic career, to say nothing of a literary one. Instruction in household arts and in the amenities of social life was thought to be sufficient for women. It was a question in many minds as to whether they were capable of assimilating knowledge of any other sort. Women were supposed to live secluded, protected and conventional lives, leaving to men the knowledge of the affairs of the world, the transaction of business and the pursuit of wisdom. To the majority of women, it must be said, this was entirely satisfactory, for they were so accustomed to have the men decide and dispose for them in all matters outside their private and narrow lives, that any attempt to throw off their shackles, to soar into the spheres of literature and art, seemed strange and unfamiliar to their natures.

But that in the seventeenth century in Spain there were women who felt the injustice of the limitations imposed upon them by a man-made world and who yearned for greater spiritual and mental development, we have only to study the career of Doña María de Zayas y Sotomayor to be rendered certain. Some of these, sure of their latent potentialities, had the moral courage, not only to protest against, but to break away from, the conventional routine and to

7

pursue the bent of their respective talents. Doña María de Zayas y Sotomayor was among the number. In the preface to the first part of her novels,[1] she gives utterance to the challenge that still rings through the ages, gradually becoming more confident, and promising to overcome all obstacles. It is a most personal touch from this author, who demands by what right men claim to be so wise and learned, and presume that women cannot be so too?[2] She condemns the wickedness and tyranny that insist on keeping women locked up and under repression, that will not give them teachers nor instruction.

" The real reason why women are not learned," she says, " is not because they lack mentality, but because they are not given the opportunity to apply themselves to study. If, in childhood, they gave us books and masters instead of lace-making and fine embroidery, we should be just as well prepared for positions of state and for professorships as are the men, and perhaps we should have more discernment, being more dispassionate in our temperaments. Our repartee is quicker, we are more carefully deliberate in our deceptions, and whatever is done with cleverness, although it be not virtue, shows creative faculty."

Little wonder that Doña María thought women capable of meddling in politics!

She continues:

"[3] And, if these reasons are not convincing and to our credit, then there will stand us in good stead the testimony of history in

[1] *Novelas Amorosas y Ejemplares:* Compuestas por Doña María de Zayas y Sotomayor. Zaragoça, 1637.

[2] " . . . q' razon ay para que ellos seā sabios, y presuman que nosotras no podemos serlo? esto no tiene, a mi parecer, mas respuesta q' su impiedad, o tirania en encerrarnos, y no darnos maestros: y, assi la verdadera causa de no ser las mugeres doctas, no es defeto del caudal, sino fata [*sic*] de la aplicacion, porque si en nuestra criança, como nos ponen el cambray en las almohadillas, y los dibuxos en el bastidor, nos dieran libros, y preceptores, fueramos tan aptas para los puestos, y para las Catedras, como los hōbres, y quiça mas agudas, por ser de narural [*sic*] mas frio, por consistir en humedad el entendimiento, como se ve en las respuestas de repente, y en los engaños de pensado, que todo lo que se haze con maña, aunque no sea virtud, es ingenio."

[3] " . . . y quando no valga esta razon para nuestro credito, valga la experiencia de las historias, y veremos por ellos lo q' hizieron las mugeres que trataron de buenas letras. De Argentaria esposa del Poeta Lucano, refiere eι mismo, que le ayudò en la correccion de los tres libros de la Farsalia, y le

regard to what women have done in the field of letters. We are told by the poet Lucan himself that his wife Argentaria helped him correct the three books of the Pharsalia, and composed many verses for him which were palmed off as his own. Themistoclea, sister of Pythagoras, wrote a most learned book of maxims. Diotima was held in great respect by Socrates. Aspasia gave many critical lectures in the Academias. Eudoxa left a book written on political science; Zenobia, an epitome of Oriental history; and Cornelia, wife of Africanus, a collection of intimate correspondence written in most elegant style. There is an infinite number of others, of antiquity and of our own times, which I pass over in silence. . . . Well then, if these things are true what reason is there why we may not show aptitude for books?"

Doña María de Zayas had an inquiring mind, alive to current events and interested in progress. She says, "Whenever I see a book, new or old, I leave my lace-making and do not rest until I have read it through. From this inclination of mine was born the knowledge I have, and from this knowledge a sense of good taste." [4]

Throughout her writings there is ever present a defensive note in condemnation of man in respect to his attitude toward woman. But this is not surprising nor undeserved, for the position of woman in the eyes of man at this particular time was not an elevated nor an enviable one. Navarrete[5] contrasts this period with the time of Queen Isabel, when women were most ambitious, and, following the example of the Queen who gave lessons to princes in the " Art of Ruling," they delved into the realm of study and were respected by the men for their learning and accomplishments. Then the University of Alcalá, recently founded and enlarged by

hizo muchos versos, que passaron por suyos. Temistoclea hermana de Pitagoras, escrivio un libro doctissimo de varias sentencias. Diotimia fue venerada de Socrates por eminente. Aspano hizo muchas leciones de opiniõ en las Academias. Eudoxa dexo escrito un libro de cõsejos politicos. Cenovia un epitome de la historia Oriental. Y Cornelia muger de Africano, unas epistolas familiares, con suma elegancia. Y otras infinitas de la antiguedad, y de nuestros tiempos, que passo en silencio. . . . Pues si esto es verdad, q' razon ay para que no tengamos prontitud para los libros." Ed. 1637, Zaragoça.

   [4] " . . . en viendo qualquiera nuevo, o antiguo, dexo la almohadilla, y no sossiego hasta que le passo. Desta inclinacion nacio la noticia, de la noticia el buen gusto."

   [5] *Bibl. de Aut. Esp.*: Novelistas post. a Cervantes.

Cardinal Cisneros, was at its height and had as its leader and professor in Philosophy and Rhetoric, Antonia Nebrija. Similar posts in other universities were filled by women, but, instead of steadily gaining in popularity, literary careers for women began to fall into disfavor, and gradually women were not tolerated in the universities. Emilia Pardo Bazán[6] speaks of this unfavorable change as a " descent which began with the last of the Austrian rulers and was wholly consummated under the rule of the Bourbons. With the corruption and decadence that fell upon Spain, the position of women was lowered—an infallible sign of the retrogression of a nation."

To what extent woman herself brought on this state of affairs, we cannot say, but it is a fact that during the first half of the seventeenth century there was an alarming laxness of morals throughout Spain,—but especially at Court. The women assumed a freedom of manner, of dress and of living that was indeed deplorable. A study of contemporary writings and a perusal of accounts by foreigners who visited the country assure us on this point. One of these writers, a Frenchman,[7] attributed the impending ruin of many of the greatest houses in Spain to the license prevalent at the time, when every man prided himself on the number of paramours he had. He was particularly impressed by the boldness and lack of reserve displayed by the women who, by their effrontery, provoked insulting remarks from the men they met. We are told that they thronged the streets at all times, flaunting their supposed charms and decked extravagantly in the most outlandish costumes made expressly to attract attention. The majority of them were not beautiful, but sought to hide their defects by the lavish use of false hair and cosmetics, often indeed in an effort to cover the ravages of small-pox.[8] So unsafe did the streets become

[6] *Biblioteca de la Mujer*, dirigida por Emilia Pardo Bazán. Tomo III. Novelas de Doña María de Zayas, p. 16.

[7] *Voyage d'Espagne*: by Antoine de Brunel. Edited by Charles Claverie in the *Revue Hispanique*, vol. 30 (1914).

[8] *Journal du Voyage d'Espagne*: by François Bertaut. Ré-édité par S. Cassan. *Revue Hispanique*, vol. 47 (1919). Francisco A. De Icaza has touched upon this phase of social life in this period in *Las Novelas Ejemplares de Cervantes. Sus críticos . . . Sus modelos literarios*, etc. Madrid, 1915, p. 214 et seq.

that any woman, however modest and honest in her intentions, if she appeared without a male escort was open to all kinds of advances and molestation. Consequently, the women of quality who conducted themselves with propriety went abroad only in carriages or else stayed at home, hearing mass in their own chapels and thus avoiding the annoyance and embarrassment often suffered by women in the churches—then the common meeting places of all classes and the favorite rendez-vous of gallants with the objects of their attentions. Husbands who wished to keep their wives from danger and away from this pernicious influence, assumed the rôle of absolute tyrants, forbidding them any liberties whatsoever, and treating them sometimes as if they were slaves, servants or mere children.[9] Small wonder that there was little encouragement for mental growth for women, and that they naturally fell into the way of believing, even they themselves, that anything beyond the purely mundane was far above their intelligence.

Although Doña María de Zayas y Sotomayor fortified herself with arguments and examples from antiquity, yet she realized that in the publication of her novels she would meet with much adverse criticism and incur the censure of those opposed to radical and unaccustomed ventures; for a literary career for women, as has been said before, was most unusual at the time. Boldly she faces her public in her note to the reader. " I have no doubt whatsoever that you will be astonished that a woman has the audacity not only to write a book, but to have it printed. . . . Who doubts, I repeat, that there will be many who attribute to sheer lunacy this justifiable hardihood of revealing to the public my scrawls, because I am a woman—which, in the opinion of some ignorant persons, is equiv-

---

[9] "Au reste, les maris qui veulent que leurs femmes vivent bien, s'en rendent d'abord si absolus, qu'ils les traitent presque en esclaves, de peur qu'ils ont qu'une honneste liberté ne les fasse émanciper au delà des loix de la pudicité, qui sont fort peu connuës et mal observées parmy ce sexe. On m'a asseuré qu'en Andalousie, les maris les traitent comme des enfants ou comme des servantes. Car quand ils prennent leur repas, s'ils les font approcher de la table, ce n'est pas pour y manger avec eux, mais pour les servir, et s'ils ne leur donnent pas cette permission, et qu'ils veuillent les tenir dans un degré de sujetion plus honneste, ils leur donnent à manger de leur table à terre, où elles sont assises sur des tapis, ou sur des carreaux a la mode des Turcs." *Voyage d'Espagne:* Antoine de Brunel. Ed. by Charles Claverie: *Revue Hispanique,* vol. 30, p. 157.

alent to a thing absolutely incompetent." [10]   She seizes every opportunity to defend her sex, admitting no inferiority nor inequality,
although her writings bear witness that she was not insensible to
the existing conditions of things.   She seeks to point out that however blameworthy a woman may be, she is nevertheless still an equal
of man:

" Anyone who is a gentleman will not consider this [book] a
novelty, nor will he censure it as folly, because, whether this stuff
of which both men and women are made be an evolution of fire and
clay or rather a composition of spirit and clod, still it is of no
nobler texture in men than in women . . . even our souls are alike,
for souls have no gender . . . Toward women there should be no
discrimination; he who does not esteem them is wicked, because
they are necessary to him, and he who insults them is an ingrate,
for he forgets the hospitality shown him in the early years of his
life." [11]

Throughout her works there is an underlying tendency that
seeks every occasion to vindicate woman against the misapprehend-
ing judgment of man.   If there were no bad men there would be
no erring women, and for every iniquitous woman there are a
hundred that are good.   Woman is ignorant of the ways and evils
of the world by reason of her upbringing.   From the very beginning her weakness is fostered, she is made dependent, no avenue
is open to her that leads to self-expression, independence and ade-
quate knowledge.   Men take full account of this, for by reason of
these limitations they are able to maintain their ascendancy and

[10] " Quien duda, lector mio, que te causará admiracion q'una muger tenga
despejo, no solo para escrivir un libro, sino para darle a la estāpa. . . . Quien
duda, digo otra vez, q'avra muchos que atribuyan a locura esta virtuosa ossadia
de sacar a luz mis borrones, siendo muger, que en opinion de algunos necios,
es lo mismo que una cosa incapaz."

[11] " . . . pero qual quiera [libro], como sea no mas de buen Cortesano, ni
lo tendra por novedad, ni lo murmurara por desatino, porque si esta materia
de que nos cōponemos los hōbres, y las mugeres, ya sea una trabaçon de fuego,
y barro, o ya una massa de espiritus, y terrones, no tiene mas nobleza en ellos,
q'en nosotras, si es una misma la sangre, los sentidos, las potencias, y los
organos, por donde se obran sus efetos, son unos mismos, la misma alma que
ellos, por que las almas ni son hombres, ni mugeres. . . . Con mugeres no ay
competencias: quien no las estima es necio, porque las á menester, y quiça las
ultraja ingrato, pues falta al reconocimiento del hospedaje que le hizieron en la
primer jornada."

prestige. They are the victors, and can afford to be magnanimous to the weaker ally. But are they so? Far from it! Ascendancy seems but one more weapon in their able hands. They take advantage of the frailty of woman, leading her on to trust their very deceitfulness. Woe unto the woman who places her faith in so insecure a vessel, for she shall indeed reap the unjust reward of her love! With music, with billets doux, with promises and presents—the very powers of Evil are out-rivaled in strategy—her favor is sought, and trustingly she accepts all, believing implicitly in the generous giver and insistent petitioner. Most earnestly does Doña María exhort women to be firm, to hold much in reserve, to remember that to give too freely is but to court a broken heart, broken vows and neglect.

The second part of the *Novelas* was written of set purpose to warn women against the mistakes which through ignorance they so often make, by revealing the pitfalls that jeopardize their happiness. She writes not to protect the willing and contented sinner, undeserving the name of woman, but to point out the snares and ambushes laid along the way for the unsuspecting victim of good intentions. She asserts that the good woman is far more unfairly treated than the irresponsible woman who does not stand by a man long enough to have him tire of her, and she emphasizes the fact that men do tire of women easily, seeking ever new conquests, never hesitating to abandon the old love for the new, with little care for the duties left unfulfilled. They are incapable of loving as deeply as does a woman. A woman's love is so great and unselfish that it stands all tests, enabling her to suffer insults, ingratitude and the sacrifice of her own good name.

Thus does Doña María excuse the frailties of woman, and thus does she enjoy depicting her. Let it be said, however, that in her zeal to present to a sympathetic public a loving and unsuspecting martyr she sometimes falls into the error of portraying a simpleton whose stupid blindness is altogether ridiculous. Sowing his wild oats, on the other hand, is no excuse for a young man's failings. Her warning is that if he does not start right, he will probably not end right. One has only to look around to be convinced that no amount of reforming after marriage will avail to change habits established in youth. Pessimistically she exclaims: " Who is the silly fool who wishes to marry, with so many pitiful examples facing her at every step? "

Men feel that women are without a fundamental moral sense, are fickle, and, as such, are not to be trusted. Whether with or without justification men are suspicious of women; and it is difficult, if not impossible, to convince them of the fact that a fine, noble woman will not stoop to deceit and baseness. Doña María tells us that so great is this prejudice that even the plays and books of the day reflect the tendency. Men's greatest amusement seems to lie in perpetrating disparaging remarks on women's infidelity. She ingeniously suggests that men are jealous and assume this attitude because secretly, in their hearts, they know that women are clever, and, if given the opportunity, might prove formidable rivals in their own fields. For this reason they want them kept stupid and pliable. In her novel, *El prevenido engañado,* she develops this idea by portraying her hero as losing faith in all women because one woman has been false to him. He believes that the more sophisticated a woman is, the better is she prepared to deceive, and consequently he goes through the world seeking a wife who shall be virtuous, good to look upon, of gentle birth (tho not necessarily rich), but whose knowledge shall not extend beyond that requisite to the care of a home, the upbringing of children and the protection of her husband's name. Otherwise—altho we are not told so in so many words—she is to be a mere clod—stupid, dull and uninteresting. He fears the well-informed, bright, intelligent woman more than he does death itself. Through the Duchess, to whom D. Fadrique discloses his views, we hear the author herself argue in favor of the intelligent woman, wise to the ways of the world, versus the stupid and ignorant fool who would never be clever enough to extricate herself from any predicament, nor quick-witted enough to save her husband's honor. What satisfaction could there be in a love founded on so shallow a foundation, for a stupid person is incapable of deep and sustained sentiment. The author cunningly arranges that the hero shall undergo an experience which changes his opinion and convinces him of the truth of this argument.

No punishment is too drastic for the man who wrongs a woman.

Her attitude is implacable on this point. She lauds the courage of the woman who avenges her honor by slaying the man who deceives her, and sincerely wishes that such justice might oftener be meted out, that men might take heed and beware of trifling with women's affections. In the novela *El imposible vencido* a married man who seeks to press his unwelcome attentions upon a respectable widow by a trick of walking through her house at night disguised as a ghost, is discovered, arrested, and condemned to die for his misdemeanor. The author's comment is simply that it is what he deserved. In spite of this apparently uncompromising attitude, we still find, depicted in the *Novelas,* some very good men who chivalrously redress the wrongs of women, who love truly, and who are faithful through all viscissitudes.

There is no sweeter love-story than that in *El desengañado amado* of the patient, generous and ideal lover D. Sancho, and Doña Clara, an example of a virtuous and long-suffering wife, to whom he is later married after the death of her husband. Although deserted by an unfaithful husband, still she remained true to him, maintaining that as God had given him to her through the vows of the church she would cleave to him and to him alone as long as he lived. D. Sancho accepts with resignation her determination, but nevertheless continues to wait patiently, watching tenderly over her from afar until the death of the husband gives him the right to renew his petition.

In all her literary work, Doña María reveals herself as an ardent Christian, to whom a religious life represents the perfect state. In her novels, after passing through the trials and tribulations of this world, it is not unusual to find the heroine entering a convent in order to escape the persecution and ill-treatment of man. There, at last, she finds true happiness and peace, and is content to remain in the shelter of the church for the remainder of her natural life.

In *Al Fin se paga todo,* the friendly protector of Doña Hipólita places her in a convent as a temporary measure, and she decides, after tasting the pleasures of a sequestered life, to remain there, refusing to return to her husband.

*La Fuerza del amor* gives us another example of a disillusioned woman taking the veil to serve God, the only true lover, who, unlike man, is ever grateful and appreciative of the love and devotion rendered him.

In *El Desengañado Amado,* when Doña Juana, who is not lead-ing an exemplary life, is warned by the ghost of a dead lover that her soul is doomed, she immediately repents, happily rejoicing in the opportunity offered her to insure for herself salvation and eternal peace.   Throughout her writings, in any case of dangerous illness, the soul receives first attention, in preparation for meeting its Maker; then, when this is accomplished, the Church makes way for the physicians, who minister to the body.   The spiritual needs, the duty of man towards his Creator, and the preparation through-out this life for the life to come—all these things are constantly emphasized.   Unlike so many writers of similar tales, never does she direct a breath of unfavorable criticism against the clergy, rather are their lives and deeds extolled and magnified.   Doña María de Zayas believed in a just retribution for transgressors, not only in the future life, but even the present one.   *Al fin se paga todo* was written expressly to demonstrate that the wicked are not immune from punishment in this world, but that before they leave it they must begin to pay for their crimes and misdeeds.

Her faith in the efficacy of prayer is illustrated by many in-stances in her novels, where the apparently impossible is brought to pass through the medium of earnest prayer.

The Moors formed so romantic an element in the Spain of her day that, like most writers of the period, she could not resist the temptation to introduce incidents wherein figure Moorish captives, Moorish princes, Moorish slaves and Moorish adventurers.   Many of these are represented as kindly, chivalrous, just and altogether humane and attractive.   Yet, at times, her staunch Catholic con-science troubles her, and we are amused to find her inventing ex-cuses for these sheep without the fold whom she was loath to condemn.   We find them about to become Christians, or open to conviction, ready to change their faith at the opportune moment. This religious attitude in the *Novelas,* together with their lofty purpose of defending the rights of woman, infuses into their extreme realism a spirit of idealism which raises them above the novels of this type current at the time.

These stories have unquestionable value in that they reflect, as in a mirror, the tendencies of the age. In the elaborate and detailed descriptions of social entertainments, artistic decorations and dress, we are better able to penetrate into the customs, the tastes and the foibles of a period which has ever been replete with interest, and, as we read, we are gradually aware that unconsciously the author wove into her narrative the spirit and atmosphere of the society in which she moved.

# CHAPTER III

## THE NOVELAS

### 1.—*General Characterization*

In spite of her adaptability, skill and manifest success in the realm of verse, the fame of Doña María de Zayas y Sotomayor rests almost wholly on her short stories. The suggestion has already been made that, notwithstanding her fearlessness, she was still uncertain as to the reception of her work by the public. Her preface to the *Novelas* is almost an apology, and is fortified in the earlier editions by a "word" from one who claims to be impartial and unbiased in his judgment. His espousal of the book is not signed, so we have no definite idea as to who this person can be, but the text of his warm recommendation would lead one to believe that the bookseller had collaborated in its rather extravagant praise. He cannot imagine anyone disliking the book or doubting in any way the marvelous and stupendous genius revealed in its pages. He is sure that the book will go down through the ages as unique of its kind and adds that even then it is the wonder of all living beings. (Is this an example of conservative advertising in the seventeenth century?) He continues in this strain, with the assurance that Genius welcomes the author with the applause due to a most remarkable woman, who stands as the Glory of Manzanares and an honor to Spain. In the *Academias* of Madrid she has been lauded as a phenix of learning! Concerning her book, the eulogist feels very strongly that the reader should not only read it but should own it. He should not borrow it, nor should he furtively read it in the book-stalls to save buying it, for that is no way to read a good book, and a very easy way to miss the good it contains. Thus a great wrong is sometimes done to both the author and the bookseller through ill-considered criticism. It is also unfair to impose on the kindness of the bookseller by borrowing it over night, to return the next day, probably in poor condition. Prospective buyers see it has been returned, are suspicious of its value, and do not buy. (Could any but the bookseller have presented his case so earnestly?) These precautions and fears were however needless, for the *Novelas* were eagerly bought and read and became very popular. In the second part of her work, published about ten years later, Doña María speaks proudly of the success of her earlier venture and of the jealousy displayed by other authors at the welcome accorded these writings from the pen of a woman.[1]

The first part of the *Novelas amorosas y ejemplares* was originally published about the year 1637 at Zaragoza, and contains the following tales: *Aventurarse perdiendo; La burlada Aminta; El castigo de la miseria; El prevenido engañado; La fuerza del amor; El desengañado amado; Al fin se paga todo; El imposible vencido; El juez de su causa; El jardín engañoso.* There is an edition of 1635 mentioned by Brunet[2] and one of 1636 mentioned by Ochoa,[3] but research seems to disprove these dates, and to justify the suggestion that these two authorities respectively mistook for the date of publication the dates of two successive Ecclesiastical Approvals— one of 1635 and the other of 1636—both of which appear in the first edition of 1637. Furthermore, the edition of 1638 and nearly all subsequent editions are advertised as "*corrected and amended*," but the edition of 1637,[4] copies of which are still extant, bears no such notice.

[1] " Que trabajos del entendimiento, el que sabe lo que es lo estima, y él que no lo sabe, su ignorancia le disculpa; como sucedió en la primera parte de este sarao, que si unos le desestimaron, ciento le aplaudieron y todos le buscaron, y le buscan, y ha gozado de tres impresiones, dos naturales, y una hurtada." Novelas amorosas y ejemplares. Paris 1847. *La Inocencia castigada,* p. 234.

[2] *Manuel du Libraire* et de l'Amateur de Livres; par Jacques-Charles Brunet. 6 vols. Paris, 1864, p. 1530, vol. v.

In *Scarron Inconnu,* by Henri Chardon, Paris 1903, the date of 1634 is given as that of the publication of the first and second parts of the work of Doña María de Zayas at Barcelona. Needless to say, this is an error, for the author herself speaks of the separate publication of the two parts of the *Novelas,* the first antedating the second by a number of years.

[3] *Tesoro de Novelistas Esp. antiguos y modernos.* Paris, 1847.

[4] *Novelas | Amorosas, y | Exemplares | Compuestas por Doña | María de Zayas y Sotomayor, na- | tural de Madrid. | Con Licencia, | En Zaragoça, En el Hospital Real, y Gñl de N. Senora | de Gracia, Año 1637. | A costa de Pedro Esquer, Mercader de libros. | 8°. Aprovacion de Maestro Joseph de Valdivielso, Madrid a 2 de Junio de 1636.—Licencia del Doctor Juan de Mendieta:

The library of the Hispanic Society of America in New York possesses, besides the edition of 1637, several editions of the *Novelas* published at Zaragoza in 1638, and one at Barcelona in 1648. In the editions thus far mentioned, only the First Part of the *Novelas* appears. In the introducion to the third novel of the Second Part of her work, Doña María states that the First Part of the novels had undergone three printings, two of these legitimate and one stolen. Leaving out of consideration the possible editions of 1635 and 1636, the authenticity of which seems dubious, we are confronted with the extant edition of 1637, two editions of 1638— all three of the foregoing printed in Zaragoza by the same bookseller—and one of 1646, printed in Barcelona. Did the author consider the two editions of 1638 as constituting one reprinting, and then that of Barcelona as the one unauthorized?[5]

The second part together with the first part of the novels appeared for the first time in 1647, according to Nicolás Antonio.[6] The novels contained in the second part are *La esclava de su amante; La mas infame venganza; La inocencia castigada; El verdugo de su esposa; Tarde llega el desengaño; Amar solo por vencer; Mal presagio casar lejos; El traidor contra su sangre; La perseguida triunfante; Estragos que causa el vicio.* Manuel Serrano y Sanz mentions an edition of 1649 not indicated elsewhere containing only the second part of the *Novelas*. No note is made as to where the book is to be found.

Madrid a 4 de Junio de 1626 [sic].—Aprovacion y licencia del Doctor D. Juan Domingo Briz, Zaragoça de Mayo de 1635.—A Doña María de Zayas, Décimas, el Dr. Joseph Adrian de Angaiz.—Décimas de María Caro de Mallén.—Redondillas de Doña Isabel Tintor, natural de Madrid.—Soneto de Doctor Iuan Pérez de Montaluan.—Soneto de D. Alonso de Castillo Solórçano.—Soneto de Francisco de Aguirre Vaca.—Décima de D. Alonso Bernardo de Quirós.—Soneto de Diego de Pereira en portugues.—Soneto de Doña Ana Inés Victoria de Mires y Arguillur.—Soneto de D. Victorian Joseph de Esmir y Casanate.—Al que leyere. Prologo de vn desapassionado.

A copy of this edition may be found in the Library of the Hispanic Society of America, and in the Ticknor Collection, Boston Public Library.

[5] C. Pérez Pastor tells us that the printers and booksellers paid very little attention to the wishes or copyright privileges of the authors. *Bibl. Madrileña*, vol. i, p. xlii.

[6] I have not succeeded in locating this edition in the catalogue or on the shelves of any library or museum.

With this exception, all the editions published after 1647 contain both the first and second parts. They are as follows: 1648, Barcelona (to be found in the British Museum); 1659, Madrid (Hispanic Society); 1664, Madrid (British Museum); 1705, Barcelona (British Museum); 1724 and 1729, Madrid (mentioned by Serrano y Sanz); 1734, Barcelona (Hispanic Society); 1748, Madrid and 1752, Barcelona (mentioned by Brunet; I can find no other mention of this edition); 1764, Barcelona (British Museum); 1786, Madrid (Hispanic Society); 1795, Madrid (British Museum); 1814, Madrid (Hispanic Society); 1847, Paris (Hispanic Society).

Some of the *Novelas* have appeared in collections which are easily accessible. There is the *Tesoro de Novelistas Españoles Antiguos y Modernos,* con una introducción y noticias de Eugenio de Ochoa, published in Paris, 1847, which contains four of the *Novelas: El Castigo de la miseria; La Fuerza del Amor; El Juez de su causa; Tarde llega el desengaño.*

The *Biblioteca de la Mujer* is a collection of selected works by various authors, edited by Emilia Pardo Bazán, for the purpose of presenting to women a library on scientific, historical and philosophical subjects best suited for the expansion of knowledge. The third volume of this series contains eight of the short stories by Doña María de Zayas. They are: *Aventurarse perdiendo; El castigo de la miseria; La fuerza del amor; El desengañado amado; La inocencia castigada; El verdugo de su esposa; El traidor contra su sangre; Estragos que causa el vicio.*

There are two collections of translations of some of the short stories into French. One appeared as early as 1656, containing six of the tales, bearing the title: *Les Nouvelles amoureuses et exemplaires per cette merveille de son siècle, Doña María de Zayas y Sotomayor, traduites de l'espagnol* par Ant. de Methel (D'Ouville); Paris, de Luynes 1656, in-8°.[7] The stories included in this collection are: *La Precaution inutile; S'aventurer en perdant; La Belle invisible, ou la Constance éprouvé (La Fuerza del amor); L'Amour*

[7] Brunet lists this collection as containing only five of the tales, but Henri Chardon in *Scarron Inconnu* quotes D'Ouville as dedicating to Mademoiselle de Mancini six stories translated from the works of Doña María de Zayas, giving titles.

*se paie avec l'amour (El juez de su causa); La Vengeance d'Aminte affrontée (La burlada Aminta); A la fin tout se paye.*

The second collection is entitled *Nouvelles de Doña María Dezayas,* traduites de l'Espagnol, Paris; G. Quinet, 1680. 3 tom. in 24°. Tr. by C. Vanel.[8] The table of contents reads: t. I: *L'heureux desespoir; Amint trahie, ou L'honneur vangé; L'avare puny.* Tome 2: *La précaution inutile; La force de l'amour; L'amour désabusé,* ou *La récompense de la Vertu; Un bienfait n'est jamais perdu.*

A German translation is mentioned in the Catalogue of the British Museum under the title, *" Die lehrreichen Erzählungen und Liebesgeschichten der Donna M. de Z. und S."* It is by Sophie Brentano in two volumes and published in Penig in 1806.[9]

In English, there seems to be only a single translation of one of the *Novelas,* and that is *The Miser Chastised* to be found in the *Spanish Novelists,* vol. ii, by T. Roscoe, 1832.

These are the acknowledged translations; there are others, however, introduced in the works of certain writers, the credit for which is not given to the original author. They appear ostensibly as the product of the translator. A comparison of the *Précaution inutile* by Scarron[10] with the *Prevenido engañado* by Doña María de Zayas shows that the two are identical, and is an instance illustrative of the unscrupulous practice of some authors.

The first part of the *Novelas* consists of a series of ten short stories purporting to be told respectively by five young men and five young women, gathered together for the Christmas holidays at the home of one of the young ladies, who is recovering from an

[8] This description is taken from the Catalogue of the Library of Congress. The notice given by Manuel Serrano y Sanz of the same book indicates that there are 5 vols. in 12°, with the date MDCLXXX. Brunet describes this work thus: " 5 part. in–12, qui se relient ordinairement en 2 vols. Cette traduction est anonyme. Barbier l'attribue à D'Ouville, en la confondant avec la précédente de 1656, qui porte le nom de Le Methel, ou de Methel; mais elle est de Vanel, ainsi que celui-ci nous l'apprend dans la dédicace de sa traduction des Alivios de Casandra, impr. à Paris, 1683, 3 tom. en 1 vol. in–12."

[9] *Trésor de Livres Rares et Précieux:* par Jean George Théodore Graesse. Dresde, 1867, vol. vi, p. 508.

[10] *Les Nouvelles tragi-comiques de M. Scarron.* Tome premier, Paris. (Ed. of 1731 consulted).

illness and is in need of entertainment. The second part of the *Novelas,* also consisting of ten stories, is a continuation of the first part in the sense that it is concerned with the same party of young people, gathered to celebrate the pre-marriage festivities of two of their number. There is a difference, however; for here only the young women narrate, and the ten tales are all occupied with relating incidents showing how women are misjudged and, in consequence, most unfairly treated by men.

There is, of course, nothing original in this manner of bringing together a number of disconnected tales by a thread of narrative. It is obviously an imitation of the method of Boccaccio in his *Decameron.* Emilia Pardo Bazán calls it a " felicitous imitation " of the great Italian novelist; and it is not surprising that Doña María de Zayas should have adopted this method, since it has always been popular, and has continued in vogue from the 14th century down to the present time. As is well known, the Italian influence was felt very early in Spain. There was always a connection with Italy through commerce and through a certain homogeneous current of sympathetic understanding. Boccaccio's writings were eagerly welcomed by the Spanish, and his tales copied wholly or in part. His influence was extensive and not in the least short lived. Dr. Bourland, in her valuable treatise[10a] on the *Decameron* in Spain, says: "To the Spanish moralists of the 15th century, Boccaccio is an authority; through Sannazaro, whose *Arcadia* goes back to Boccaccio's *Ameto,* he is the founder of the Pastoral Novel in Spain, while the Spanish Sentimental Novel springs directly from him." At first, Boccaccio was better known in Spain through his works other than the *Decameron,* such as the *Fiammeta,* the *Corbaccio, Caída de Principes,* etc. These exercised a certain literary influence, but the *Decameron* later surpassed them all in its deeper and more far-reaching effects. Although this work was translated into Spanish as early as 1496 (edition of Sevilla), yet its influence was not strongly felt until the middle of the sixteenth century in the *Coloquios Satíricos* of Antonio de Torquemada (1553) and the *Patrañuelo* of Juan de Timoneda (1566)—an influence which reached its apogee in the seventeenth century. In re-telling and imitating these Italian tales the Spanish adapted them to their new surroundings, infused into them the Spanish atmosphere and made them far more romantic and adventurous than the originals.  At the same time, the idea of the framework used in the *Decameron* was closely followed, but with just enough variation to distinguish the adaptations from the original.

Among the illustrations of this influence the following may be noted.  Lucas Hidalgo in his *Carnestolendas de Castilla* (1605) has interwoven his tales into an account of Carnival festivities.—In *El Pasajero* (1617), by Suarez de Figueroa, stories are told in the interludes of a journey made by two travellers; Salas Barbadillo, in *La Casa del Placer honesto* (1620), tells of four students of the University of Salamanca who, tired of their studies, set up an establishment in Madrid, where they entertain their friends and guests with various sorts of diversion, most important of which is the recounting of short stories.—Francisco Lugo y Davila, in his work entitled *Novelas morales* (1622), uses the device of three friends amusing themselves by taking turns in narrating stories during the tiresome afternoons.

*The Cigarrales of Toledo* (1624) by Tirso de Molina consists of a collection of tales, plays and poems presented by the different members of a party of friends who are seeking entertainment at several *cigarrales* or country seats near Toledo.  The device is similar to that adopted in the *Novelas* of Doña María de Zayas in that the entertainments are in turn under the leadership of various members of the assembled company.—Alonso de Castillo Solórzano has also followed the accustomed plan in his *Tardes entretenidas* (1626), *La Huerta de Valencia, Los Alivios de Casandra* (1640), *Jornadas alegres* (1626), and *La Quinta de Laura* (1649) where a number of young ladies are met at Laura's country house and amuse themselves and each other by telling stories.— Even Juan Pérez de Montalban yielded to the fashion.  In his *Para Todos* (1632), a country house is made the scene for the narrating of short stories, the presentation of plays, and the discussion of scientific subjects.

The *Auroras de Diana* (1632) by Pedro de Castro y Anaya is so called because the stories are related in the morning for the amusement of Diana, a lady of the court, who is in the country recovering from an illness.—In the prologue to his *Novelas ejemplares,* Cervantes states his intention of writing a book to be called *Semanas del Jardín,* a work of which, unfortunately, nothing further is known. Owing to his closely following death, it is probable that he never wrote it. However, his intention is significant in that it indicates that he, too, who prided himself on his originality and affected to scorn the various imitations of the *Decameron,*[11] was himself influenced to consider this form of prose fiction, which at the time was the current type of popular novel.

Small wonder that Doña María regaled her public with what the public desired. However, let it be said to her credit that, although adopting, and adapting to her use, some of the plots of the *Decameron,* yet she manifests an effort to refrain from utilizing its substance and seeks her sources elsewhere or essays to draw upon her own creative genius. In giving to the *Novelas amorosas* the descriptive title of *ejemplares,* she was doubtless following the example of Cervantes, who, desirous of distinguishing his work from the many licentious imitations of Boccaccio with which Europe was overrun during the sixteenth and the first half of the seventeenth centuries, qualified them as exemplary and moral. The novels of Doña María de Zayas are sprightly and sometimes a little crude, but scarcely objectionable enough to be termed licentious. Whatever adverse criticism has been bestowed upon them in this respect should be regarded as undeserved. Doña María is justified by the loftiness of her underlying purpose, namely, the enlightenment of her sex, and by her effective protest against the tyranny of man and the warning note she sounds to women to beware of the snares and temptations of the world. They must be judged in accordance with the period in which they were written. A study of contemporary life and letters will furnish the correct perspective. In such a survey, a certain superficial crudeness and grossness is observable in the morals of the time and in the subjects openly discussed in society, subjects that imply a somewhat startling contrast with the standards of a later day.

[11] " Yo soy el primero que he novelado en lengua castellana; que las muchas novelas que en ella andan impresas todas son traducidas de lenguas estrangeras, y estas son mias propias, no imitadas ni hurtadas; mi ingenio las engendró y las parió mi pluma, y van creciendo en los brazos de la estampa." Prologue to the *Novelas ejemplares.*

## 2.—*El Jardín engañoso*

Like the majority of writers of this period, as has been intimated, Doña María de Zayas found the sources of some of her novels in the Italian writers then so popular, foremost among them Boccaccio. This is well illustrated in her tenth story of the first part of the *Novelas,* which bears the title *El Jardín engañoso* (The Magic Garden). Florence Nightingale Jones in her study of *Boccaccio and His Imitators* states that this tale has its origin in the fifth novel of the tenth day of the *Decameron.*[12] Boccaccio, however, had already told the same story with slight variations in his *Filocolo,* in the *Thirteen Questions of Love.* It is Question IV in the fourth book. As has been stated, others of Boccaccio's works than the *Decameron* were familiar to the Spanish, and there might be very reasonable doubt as to whether Doña María de Zayas drew from the *Decameron* or from the *Filocolo.*[13] A careful examination of the three tales concerned, however, suggests that she was influenced by both.

In the story as it is told in the *Decameron,* Dianora, the wife of Gilberto, is loved by Ansaldo, whose attentions are a source of annoyance and embarrassment to her. Wishing to dispose of this unwelcome suitor, she makes what she considers an impossible demand, promising, upon its accomplishment, to yield to his courtship. He is to present her in the month of January with a garden which shall be as lovely, luxuriant and complete as if the season were the month of May. In default of this, he must desist from his attentions; otherwise she will openly denounce him to her husband and her friends.

Nothing daunted, the perplexed lover seeks out a magician who on the first day of January is able to construct in a meadow near the city a beautiful garden, that is even more wonderful than the lady had imagined. From it he sends fruits and flowers to Dianora, begging her to go and view it for herself, and reminding her of the promise she had made him. In company with her ladies, Dianora visits the enchanted spot; with sorrow and amazement she realizes that she has indeed placed herself in an apparently inextricable

[12] Univ. Chicago, 1910.
[13] May be read in Spanish in *Las treze questiones.* Toledo 1549.

predicament. In contrition she relates all to her husband. At first he is angry with her, but then, reflecting that her intentions had been upright, his mood softens and he simply chides her for having made any sort of covenant, reminding her that with lovers nothing is impossible. Because she has given her word he insists upon her keeping it, and sends her to Ansaldo's house in fulfilment of her promise. Reluctantly she follows his commands and presents herself before the man who had succeeded in overcoming supposedly insuperable obstacles. However, when Ansaldo learns that it is Dianora's husband who has sent her to him, he marvels at such generosity and, moved by the noble act, finds himself unable to accept so great a sacrifice. Instead, he sends Dianora back to her husband, vowing that he will not take advantage of such magnanimity. Through this dénouement, the ties of a deep friendship are cemented between the two men, who perceive in each other traits of extraordinary nobility and generosity of character. The magician, not to be outdone in these qualities, refuses to accept any remuneration for his labors. [The story is followed by the question as to the generosity of Ansaldo as compared with that of the hero of another tale.]

This is the story as it stands in the *Decameron*. Doña María was not satisfied simply to translate the story, but, as was the custom with the Spanish adapters of the Italian *Novelle,* she elaborated the theme, and so successfully localized the setting, adding or omitting incidents and characters and introducing manners and customs typical of her own country, that she completely transplanted the story into Spanish literature, and so imbued it with the peculiar atmosphere of the land that it seems quite naturally to belong there. In her version of the *Magic Garden* we find all the tendencies of the literature of the time. In her elegance of style and expression is indicated the influence of Góngora, while in the predominant interest of action and adventure we become aware of the negligence in character portrayal which is so typical of the period. In these transplanted bits of fiction there is an added interest in the exploitation of much that is chivalrous, romantic and heroic, much that is imaginative and fanciful. Doña María has transferred the action to Zaragoza, a city which she extols in extravagant metaphor.

This seems to have been the general manner of beginning these short stories. Whatever city was chosen as the stage for action was the " finest and the best, the jewel that twinkled brightest in the crown of Castile." It was as if these innovators composed by formula.[14] The procedure is almost always the same. Interest in the introduction of minute details is illustrated by the fact that instead of plunging directly into the story, as did Boccaccio when he related that " a worthy lady, named Dianora, the wife of a very agreeable man and one of great wealth, called Gilberto, had taken the fancy of a great and noble lord, called Ansaldo," Doña María de Zayas takes the pains to explain the parentage, with all its attendant incidents, of the heroine of the story. Constanza is her name, and that of her sister, Teodosia. Here, in the addition of the sister, is an example of elaboration of the original theme—a subtheme, as it were, that forms an integral part of the narrative. D. Jorge falls in love with Constanza and his brother Federico with Teodosia. Teodosia is indifferent to Federico but interested in D. Jorge. Her jealously adds more intricacy to the plot in that she succeeds in making trouble between her sister and her chosen lover by intimating to him that Constanza and Federico have a secret bond between them. In jealous rage, D. Jorge kills his brother Federico and embarks for Naples in flight. The death of the father of the two girls shortly afterwards leaves them in possession of considerable wealth. With time, Constanza gradually overcomes the disappointment and sorrow of her lover's unexplained desertion. When a visiting nobleman takes up his residence across the street from her home, and, smitten by her charms, seeks to win her love, she is willing to be courted by the amiable stranger. The latter, however, more noble than wealthy, is clever enough to overcome his lack of fortune through stratagem. He courts the mother's favor until he is assured of her interest, then, with the connivance of a physician, he pretends a mortal illness from which it seems unlikely that he can recover. When his life is despaired of, he calls Constanza's mother to his bedside to beg her permission to bequeath all his possessions to her daughter, with whom he is in love. The mother

[14] Consult *Las Novelas Ejemplares de Cervantes: Sus críticos,* etc., by Francisco A. de Icaza.   Madrid 1915, p. 257.

consents and the sum of 100,000 ducats is willed to Constanza. The mother, who is pleased with the young man's personality and the wealth he professes to have, mourns with her daughter that so estimable and eligible a young man should die. He does not die, however, but gradually begins to recuperate in health until he is entirely well, when he marries the object of his affections without encountering any opposition. After his marriage, he confesses his deception, but so deep is his wife's love for him that she forgives him freely, rejoicing in the happiness they enjoy together. As the years progress, two sons are added to their felicity, and the family live in ideal peace and contentment.

Meanwhile, D. Jorge learning through various channels that he has never been suspected of the murder of his brother, returns to his native city. With his return, he renews his attentions to Constanza, whom he has never forgotten.

At this point begins the tale as Boccaccio relates it but with the added complication of Teodosia's renewed jealousy, which affects her so strongly that she falls dangerously ill. Constanza, realizing the cause, is anxious to have D. Jorge marry her sister, but his thoughts and desires centre on Constanza and with ever increasing fervor he pleads with her to regard him with favor. Then follow, as in the *Decameron,* the promise and the proposition of the garden. Instead of hiring a magician as did Ansaldo, the rejected suitor meets a stranger who divines his dilemma and suggests that as long as Constanza puts a price upon her love the case is not so hopeless as it seems. He reveals himself as the Devil—a noteworthy addition by our Spanish author—who in exchange for D. Jorge's soul promises to help him solve his problem. The contract is drawn up in writing and duly signed. There are interpolations by the author concerning the mortal sin involved in bartering to the Arch Enemy the precious soul which cost its Maker so dearly. Here we have the introduction of the religious element so conspicuously absent from the original story. During the night Constanza's garden is transformed into such a paradise as is described in the *Decameron.* Carlos, the husband, is the first to view the fairy spectacle. His exclamations of astonishment bring Constanza to the scene. The realization of its meaning overwhelms her with despair, and she swoons. Upon her recovery, she confesses all to her husband, begging him to kill her, since, as a Christian, she cannot take her own life as he would wish to do, while he, as her husband, can act to save his honor. He chides her for having placed a price on what has no price, but does not denounce her, aware that she meant all for the best. Instead, he offers to kill himself to clear the situation, "forgetting that by so doing he would forfeit his soul." D. Jorge, who is present, having arrived at daybreak to view the garden, prevents him from committing so revolting a crime, explaining that he will be the only one to die, as he has already lost his soul—which had cost God his death on the cross—through a pact made with the Devil. The continual introduction of Catholic principles and religious fervor is characteristic of the work of this author.

At this juncture, the Devil appears, and, not to be surpassed in generosity, releases D. Jorge from his contract, returning to him the document, "so that the world may see with amazement that in the Devil there can be virtue." This accomplished, there is heard a loud crash, and, coincident with it, the Devil and garden disappear. D. Jorge sinks upon his knees in prayer, the rest of the company following his example and all giving thanks to God for their fortunate deliverance from evil. D. Jorge, deeply moved, begs forgiveness of Constanza for all the unhappiness he has caused her and agrees to marry Teodosia as she desires. Thus all is satisfactorily arranged and, in token of her forgiveness, Constanza throws her arms around D. Jorge's neck, welcoming him into her family as a brother. Gay festivities crown this happy ending. The two families live many years in harmony and peace, blest by beautiful children and prosperity. Until after D. Jorge's death, when Teodosia reveals the truth, nobody ever discovers that he was the murderer of his brother. Moreover, at the end of the story we are told that this tale of the *Magic Garden* was found after Teodosia's death written by her hand and designating a prize—the laurel of wisdom—for the one who shall decide which of the three was most virtuous, Carlos, D. Jorge or the Devil. After some discussion the assembled company of young men and young women agree that the Devil, without any doubt, was the one to whom most praise was due, because it is an unheard-of thing for him to do good.

This development of the outline given by Boccaccio, into something more elaborate, detailed and finished, is typical of all the adaptations by Doña María de Zayas y Sotomayor. She knew how to expand her theme so as to include in an intelligent and consistent manner an interesting variety of incidents and romantic adventures—an element so dear to the heart of Spaniards.

The story as found in the *Filocolo* is very similar to that of the *Decameron.* It varies simply in a few details. Instead of hiring a magician, Tarolfo, the lover, searches through strange lands to find some way of accomplishing the apparently impossible feat, but nowhere does he discover a means of success. Almost in depair, he is ready to give up the quest when one morning in a lonely walk which brings him to the foot of a mountain, he meets with an elderly man, bearded, small of person and thin, with clothes that mark him as being rather poor. He is gathering herbs and digging roots. In the exchange of courtesies and inquiries, the hermit learns of Tarolfo's great desire. (The idea of the meeting of Tarolfo and the hermit in the woods is adopted in *El Jardín engañoso* by Doña María.) After a few moments of silence the hermit asks him what he would give to have his wish fulfilled. Tarolfo assures him that when the work is done he may have one half of his worldly goods. The stranger agrees to undertake the task, and gathering up his belongings accompanies Tarolfo. The garden is created. There is an interesting and beautiful account of the prayer made to the different elements of nature by the creator of the garden. His invocation is almost dithyrambic in its eloquence. It seems strange that if this version of the story was familiar to Doña María de Zayas, she did not include this particular idea in her narrative as enhancing its many poetical aspects.

Unlike the procedure of the tale in the *Decameron,* the lady, instead of appealing to her husband at once, promises to favor Tarolfo if he will wait until a more propitious occasion when her husband shall have gone hunting or have left the city. To this Tarolfo agrees, but so greatly is the lady disturbed in mind that her husband perceives her perturbation and persuades her to reveal the cause of it. The succeeding events are similar to those occurring in the story of the *Decameron,* the hermit refusing to accept the reward promised him. In the final discussion as to who showed most magnanimity, the husband is conceded the honor.

Unlike his usual attitude, Boccaccio depicts his heroine with an inclination to be virtuous and to fulfil her agreement, but Doña María de Zayas, with her characteristic loyalty to the feminine sex, goes much farther, portraying her sympathetically as inherently good, loyal to her husband, a devout Catholic and ready to die for the sake of her honor and that of her family. She is given an exalted position, clothed in a garb of idealism and presented as devoid of unworthy impulses.

The diffusion of Boccaccio's tales was infectious. Many writers succumbed to a veritable epidemic of retelling them wholly or in fragments, adapting them to their own use as best pleased them. This was the case in Italy itself, as well as in foreign countries in which the editions from Italy penetrated. This particular tale, however, does not seem to have found its way into the Italian *novelle,* if the results may be trusted of an examination of the contents of those immediately following the works of Boccaccio and preceding the tales of Doña María de Zayas.[15] As A. C. Lee has correctly stated, there are several to be found which recount acts of unusual generosity of conduct, courtesy and liberality, but to the present writer it seems that none of these are similar enough to *El Jardín engañoso* to serve as a possible source for its plot.[16] Consequently it is probable that Doña María de Zayas was not influenced even indirectly by these authors, but rather drew directly from the original source, owing to the fact that Boccaccio enjoyed greater popularity than did any of the other writers and was more eagerly read.

As to the origin of the story, it must be remembered in the first place that during the Middle Ages many tales from antiquity, originating in many climes, lost their identity by free circulation and became common property. Little in the *Decameron* is new, as has

---

[15] "There does not seem to be any very direct imitation of this story in the Italian novellieri, although there are some similar ones of magnanimity." A. C. Lee, The *Decameron:* its sources and analogues. London 1909, p. 328.

[16] The stories by Gentile Sermini, Bandello and Ilicini, as mentioned by A. C. Lee, are different in theme from *El Jardín engañoso,* agreeing only in the discussion at the end concerning the one showing the most magnanimity.

often been proved. There are those who are disposed to overlook all the significant value of Boccaccio's work, content to dismiss it lightly by branding it as a mass of plagiarism. These critics of narrow vision are unmindful of the monumental and incomparable work of the master mind who saved for posterity this wealth of lore and by his manner of narration inaugurated the modern novel.

Manni intimates soberly that the story is founded on fact, and that in the year 876 a Hebrew physician by enchantment created just such a garden as is described by Boccaccio.[17] However true this may be, it is difficult to prove. Mr. Manni has been accused of a mania for founding on fact all of Boccaccio's tales, and as this tendency is indeed noticeable in his work, perhaps it is well in the present case to leave the question open. It may be added that in another account the year 1395 is given as the date of the occurrence.[17a]

That the tale is of oriental origin has been demonstrated by A. C. Lee, who in his able work has gathered together a number of versions through which it can be traced back to the story of a young girl, daughter of a wealthy merchant, who while walking in her garden spies a rose that no one seems able to procure for her. The gardener performs the difficult task, asking as a reward that she meet him in the garden on the evening of her wedding day.

[17] " Della derivazione del presente racconto sia la fede presso di uno Scrittore anonimo si, ma, che non è credibile, che abbia posto in campo una falsità alloraquando diè a leggere in difesa di Giovanni Boccaccio (indirizzandola a persone di autorità) quella Scrittura, di cui ho io fatto parola di sopra nella Giornata III. Novella II. en stente nel Codice 861. in quarto della famosa Libreria Stroziana. Imperciocchè ivi si viene a dire: *che quell' altro facesse nel Frivoli un Giardino nel cuor del Verno per incanto; la qual Novella si legge antica altrove.* Questo è peravventura quell' istesso, che da persona letteratissima di fuori mi è stato per lettera scritto cioè, *che Giovanni Tritemio racconta, come nell' 876. un tal Sedecia Medico Ebreo fece comparire alla presenza di molti gran Signori nell' Inverno un orto amenissimo con alberi. e fiori ec, come fece a Messere Ansaldo il Negromante.* Sul fatto poi di sopra mentovato di Buonaccorso Pitti, che tentò per amore di far cosa difficile molto, si legge nell' Annotazioni alla Cronica di esso: *Cosi M. Dianora chiese a M. Ansaldo un giardino di Gennaio bello come di Maggio.*"—Istoria del Decamerone di Giovanni Boccaccio, scritta da Domenico Maria Manni. Firenze. M. DCC. XXXXII. [In line *1* of this note, *sia* should perhaps read *si a;* and in line 5, *en stente* should probably read *esistente*.]

[17a] A. C. Lee gives the reference as Muratori, ' Scriptores,' vol. xix, p. 398; Borromeo, 32; Gamba bibl. 30; but says the chronicler is anonymous.

With her bridegroom's consent she goes to fulfil her word, and on the way encounters in turn a wolf and a robber, both of whom, after being informed of her promise, allow her to proceed on her errand.  The gardener, on learning of the thrice repeated magnanimity of bridegroom, wolf and robber, does not detain her, but permits her in peace to return to her husband.  This version, according to Lee, is found in the preparations of the *Cukasaptati* and in the *Guti-nameh,* written by Nakhshabi about 1306.  The subsequent versions found in other Oriental works,[18] and later with slight variations in French fables, are similar to this version.  The story is usually told with the object of discovering, through the comments made upon the comparative sense of honor of the characters, who the thief is among a number of suspected persons.

Boccaccio took his material where he found it, arranged it to suit himself, and retold it with such originality that it read as freshly as if never related before.  This is true of the story of Ansaldo and Dianora in the *Decameron* or that of Tarolfo in the *Filocopo.*  In his version of the story we trace the skeleton of the original, which consisted in the accomplishment of a difficult feat together with an act of extraordinary magnanimity, and the attendant question as to which of the characters involved was the most generous.  The rest he filled in himself, apparently being the first to employ the incident of the magic garden, which Doña María de Zayas borrowed *in toto.*[19]

[18] *Baitál Pachisí; Kathá sarit Ságara; Bahar-Danush; Thousand and One Nights* etc., p. 322 et seq.

[19] Imitations of Boccaccio's story given by Miss Jones in her book, *Boccaccio and his Imitators,* are:

    1387 Chaucer: Franklin's Tale.
    1459 Johann Valentin: Andrae's Chymische Hochzeit " Christiani Rosencreutz."
    1470 Bojardo: Orlando Innamorato. Canto XII. " Iroldo e Tisbina."
    1536 Nicolas de Troyes, Parangon: " Le Jardin de Janvier."
    1567 Painter, " Palace of Pleasure: Ansaldo and Dianora."
    1608 Beaumont and Fletcher: Triumph of Honor.
    1620 Two Merry Milkmaids.
    1637 María de Zayas—" El Jardín Engañoso."

### 3.—*El Castigo de la miseria*

Avarice is a despicable trait and has always been a popular subject with writers of fiction, just as has been its counterpart, the trait of liberality, in all ages and in all countries. A miser is despised, and any trick or any deceit to defraud him of his money is accounted justifiable and laudable. A long list could be made of novels in which the trait of liberality has been the principal subject. Doña María de Zayas availed herself of this theme and produced what has been regarded as her best-constructed story. It is the third novel of Part One.

D. Marcos, from the kingdom of Navarre, is a man of good birth and lofty ideals, but with no money to support them. At the age of twelve and entirely without funds, he comes to Court to serve one of the nobles. At first he battles through many hardships, but manages to keep himself alive and by hoarding gradually accumulates a small sum of money, which increases with the years. Sometimes he almost starves, for his wages are small and he endeavors to save every cent that comes into his possession. This habit of thrift becomes a mania, and, although better paid when later on he assumes the office of page, yet he continues to live in as niggardly a manner as before. He begs water from the water-carriers or wine from the servants carrying it past the house; he uses the candle stubs that people throw away, or else undresses for bed in the dark. He eats from his companions' plates and this manner of providing for his meals becomes such a habit that when they see him coming they swallow all at one mouthful or cover the food in their plates with their hands. When traveling, the provender for his horse is often furnished by the straw in the mattress. The boy he has for a servant is treated hardly better than his horse. With all this scrimping and saving, D. Marcos manages to add to his pile, and in time gains the reputation at Court of being wealthy. At the age of thirty he has accumulated a small fortune of six thousand ducats, which he carries with him everywhere for fear of being robbed.

In spite of his besetting sin, D. Marcos has good habits and is considered a fine catch. But he turns down all the opportunities offered him to marry, until urged by a professional matchmaker to consider a certain Doña Isidora, a widow professing to be worth thirteen or fourteen thousand ducats, but really an adventuress. D. Marcos is simple-minded and gullible, and the lady's fortune and the lavish comfort of her household make an impression on him. He is entertained so lavishly that when urged by the matchmaker to venture a proposal he is nothing loath. His suit is favored and he is duly accepted. The marriage takes place with much attendant pomp and splendor. The groom enthusiastically marvels how the Fates have been so kind; but once installed with Doña Isidora in her home, his dreams of peace, happiness and accumulated riches quickly pass. The awakening is rude. The very first night the gold chain he prizes so highly and the wedding finery for which he has so reluctantly and begrudgingly spent some of his savings, are stolen by one of the servants. In the early morning hours he awakes in response to the outcry made upon discovery of the outer door wide open, and is not so taken aback at all the excitement as he is to behold his wife minus the many accessories to her toilet with which she is wont to cover the ravages of time and of which poor D. Marcos had not the faintest suspicion. The next calamity comes in the form of a request that the silver plate be returned to its owner, from whom it has been borrowed. Protests on the part of D. Marcos avail little. He is beginning to realize that he has been duped, and that his wife is not all she seemed. He threatens divorce and other means of redress. His wife tries to quiet him by the assurance that to win such a husband a little deception is forgivable. But peace is short-lived, for the man from whom the furniture and draperies have been rented comes to collect payment on the same, and finally goes off with the articles. This is too much for D. Marcos; turning to his wife, he lays hands upon her that are none too gentle. The uproar brings down the owner of the house, who lives in an upper room. He announces that he is a lover of peace, and if they intend to continue their daily quarrels they will oblige him by moving elsewhere. Poor D. Marcos! He has been led to believe that the house belongs to his wife. It is not long before he knows how basely he has been deceived. He seeks new quarters for himself and wife. While absent from the house, Doña

Isidora and her paramour, whom she has introduced to D. Marcos as her nephew and who forms part of the family, pack all the household goods into carts and together with the servant start on their way to Barcelona. When D. Marcos discovers this perfidy and that his money also has been taken, he almost loses his mind. In desperation, wondering where he is to procure the means to pay the cost of the wedding, he turns in the direction of his patron's house. On the way there, he comes face to face with Marcela, the maid who had disappeared the night of the wedding with his gold chain and finery. Upon her as a last hope he pounces, demanding the return of the stolen articles. Marcela, in tears, protests that everything is in the possession of his wife, who planned the theft but let her servant shoulder the blame. D. Marcos, who is of a trusting disposition and without malice, believes the girl, and in turn confides to her the misfortune that has befallen him and his desire to learn the whereabouts of Doña Isidora and her nephew. Marcela, cunning in her knowledge of the poor man, offers to help him by introducing him to a magician who is endowed with marvellous occult powers. D. Marcos eagerly seizes the opportunity and a rendez-vous is arranged. The advance payment for the séance he is obliged to borrow, for he is well-nigh penniless. At the stipulated hour, D. Marcos presents himself. He is taken into a dimly lighted room, where as the impostor reads incantations from an old book (which is nothing less than the *Amadís de Gaula*), a cat, put in training for the purpose, is set on fire, and scared through a cat-hole into the room, and leaps scratching and squalling over D. Marcos' head through a window directly above him, burning his hair and whiskers in its mad flight. D. Marcos faints dead away, believing he sees not one demon but a whole flaming inferno of them. The commotion is so great that people rush in to see what the trouble is. The magician and Marcela, his accomplice, are arrested, and the deception practised on D. Marcos is disclosed. Upon his recovery D. Marcos makes his way to his master's home, where a note is awaiting him from Doña Isidora denouncing him roundly for his avarice and promising that she will return to him when he shall again have gathered together six thousand ducats. So great is his rage, and the blow to his pride occasioned by the public disgrace, that he contracts a fever and dies within a few days.  Doña Isidora, however, receives her just deserts, for, soon afterwards, her so-called nephew and the maid take the six thousand ducats and all her possessions and embark for Naples in each other's company.  Doña Isidora, putting aside her wig and her many embellishments, is forced to resort to begging.  The tale is told as a warning to niggards.

Unlike *El Jardín engañoso,* no precursor of *El Castigo de la miseria* is found in the *Decameron.*  An inspection of Boccaccio's work reveals only two novels that treat in any way of avarice.  In novel seven of the first day, Bergamino by telling a clever story reproves the avarice which has lately appeared in the rich Messer Cane della Scala's manner of entertaining his guests.  In novel eight of the first day, there is told the story of a certain M. Ermino de Grimaldi who, although extremely wealthy, is yet noted for his greediness and sordid avarice.  By a witty retort, Gulielmo Borsieri puts him to shame and thus works a complete change in his disposition.  Hardly can it be said that the short story by Doña María de Zayas bears any connection with these two tales.

An examination of the *Piacevoli Notte* by Straparola (first half of the sixteenth century), whose works were enjoyed and imitated in Spain, discloses nothing significant.  Fable thirteen of night thirteen tells of a wealthy man noted for his prodigality who loses all his money and is promptly deserted by those to whom he has been most generous in his days of plenty.  One day he finds in a ruined hut an earthen vessel filled with ducats.  Instead of returning to his former mode of living, he becomes most niggardly and is loath to share his find with anyone.  There seems little again in this tale to warrant comparison with *El castigo de la miseria.*

Nor is there apparently any source for the story in Bandello's *Novelle* nor in the tales by Cinthio, both of which writers were popular in Spain.

Let us turn next in our quest to the fiction in Spain preceding the writing of the novel in question.  In the *Patrañuelo* (1576) of Juan de Timoneda, the first collection of stories in Spain to show the influence of the *Decameron,* there is related the tale of a blind man (*patraña* twelve) who has all the characteristics of a miser.

He deprives himself of necessaries, saves religiously all the money he can lay his hands on, and spends his evenings counting and fondling the precious coin. A neighbor, taking in the situation through a peephole in the miser's shed, enters the hut and steals the money. Great is the lament of the blind man upon discovery of the theft. The next morning, on his way to report to the authorities, he meets another blind man, to whom he relates his misfortune. The newcomer in answer boasts that no one can steal his money, for he carries it safely in the lining of his cap. The robber, who from curiosity is lingering near, hears this, and snatching the bonnet from the old man's head runs away with it. Blind man number two, believing that blind man number one has taken the cap, begins to beat him. The other retaliates, while the robber makes good his escape.—The similarity is too slender for our purpose.

In the *Corrección de vicios* (1623), by Alonso Jerónimo de Salas Barbadillo, there is depicted a deplorable example of avarice, a miserly merchant the list of whose mean economies approaches the incredible; and yet, in this characterization there is something suggestive of D. Marcos. Doña María, however, has clothed her hero with more respectability and a touch of human sentiment, while the miser of Salas Barbadillo is a clod, who inspires us with loathing and disgust. To save bed-linen, he sleeps on a board and uses a stone for a pillow; he does all his own work, being devoid of the pride that impels D. Marcos to attach to himself a servant— no matter how humble nor how inefficient—to perform the menial tasks of the household. Like D. Marcos he undresses at night in the dark to save candle light and when in the house during the day wears his clothes very loosely or takes them off entirely in order to avoid wear and tear. Again like D. Marcos, he is pictured as depending for his food on crusts from his neighbors or the extraction of tid-bits from their plates; and yet there is the difference that D. Marcos never assumes a cringing or servile attitude, but follows his unfortunate bent with the abstracted air of a gentleman. Salas Barbadillo has so exaggerated the character of his miser that as a whole he lacks reality. Even in his last illness, with death staring him in the face, he eschews medicine, unwilling to spend the small sum that might have brought him relief. Upon his death, his brother and brother's family, whom he has seen suffering before his eyes from poverty without ever proffering them aid, inherit the old man's savings of 20,000 ducats and enjoy the comfort the hoàrder never knew.

It is very probable that Doña María was familiar with the above work and in its perusal assimilated some of the ideas therein contained in preparation for delineating the pet economies displayed by D. Marcos, but there is much more likelihood that she may have been influenced by *El casamiento engañoso* of Cervantes, which forms one of his *Novelas ejemplares*—published in 1613, but, according to Icaza, probably composed about 1605. *El casamiento engañoso* resembles the novela of Doña María de Zayas in that the *alférez* Campuzano is taken in by an adventuress whom he has met by chance and who presents a most attractive exterior, having an air of distinction and elegance that to the enamored gentleman is altogether captivating. In addition to her personal charms, she has the air and appearance of being in most comfortable circumstances, and it is not until after marriage that the *alférez* discovers that he has indeed been deceived and that the fine establishment he was led to believe to be hers really belongs to a friend who was absent on a visit and has only been availed of to accomplish the purpose of baiting a husband—that in fact his wife has nothing. Forced to move to other lodgings, he returns home one day to discover that his wife, in company with a man she has called her cousin, has deserted him, taking with her all her husband's belongings—including his massive jewelry—and has left him nothing but a travelling suit. Happily, the jewelry which appeared to be gold is only brass; for the husband, too, has been playing at the same game. Poetic justice accomplishes its ends in the outcome. In the development of the plot, there is the same atmosphere and portrayal of society and manners which is found to be later so characteristic of the tales of Doña María.

Francisco de Icaza in his critical study of this novel refers to an interesting and curious account of the Court of Spain in 1605 given by Dr. Thomé Pinheiro de Vega, a Portuguese who visited Spain in this period and whose description of the indiscriminate and unscrupulous conduct of the people of the Court stamps certain events in *El casamiento engañoso* as true to life. Yet in this novel by Cervantes, although the *alférez* marries in order to come into possession of a comfortable living, the idea of avarice and sordid penury is not touched upon. Here there is no figure that stands out as does D. Marcos, around whose mania for economizing the plot develops. In short, there is no character development such as is found in *El castigo de la miseria*. If Doña María was inspired by Cervantes, it was only in connection with the marriage of the *alférez* to the adventuress with the resulting circumstances. She has so embellished this episode and added so much else of marked value that her debt to Cervantes indeed seems negligible.

Still another more primitive source suggested for *El casamiento engañoso* is the famous *Aulularia* of Plautus—utilized by Molière in his *l'Avare*. So far as we know, this play was not translated into Spanish until recently, when an excellent translation was made by Dr. A. Gonzalez Garbín.[20] According, however, to Cotarelo y Morí,[21] the subject of this Latin play was not unknown in Spain, and it is possible that Doña María was familiar with the story of the Athenian Euclio who all his life has been miserably wretched and poor, until he finds an earthen vessel filled with gold hidden under the hearth of his fire. Instead of being overjoyed at this find and putting it to good use, he carefully hides it, and from that moment becomes a most unhappy being, unable to sleep for fear of thieves and loath to leave his home by day. He continues in his poverty, zealously watching his treasure, guarding his secret and suspicious of everybody. When Megadorus, a wealthy neighbor, asks Euclio for his daughter in marriage, the miser is at once distrustful, and believes Megadorus would not consider a poor girl like Phaedra unless he suspected that Euclio has hidden wealth. He stoutly maintains he is so poor that he cannot give his daughter a dowry, and is puzzled and nonplussed to find that to Megadorus all this seems immaterial. Finally, under his own conditions, he consents to the marriage, which is to take place that very day. He is unaware that Phaedra already has a lover in the person of Lyconides, nephew to

---

[20] *Teatro de Plauto. Traducción y comentario de las principales comedias. Por A. Gonzales Garbín. Granada, 1879.*
[21] *Estudios de Historia Literaria de España,* etc.

Megadorus, and that she is bound to him through their secret intimacy.

As events progress the suspicions of Euclio, instead of diminishing, increase. The fear that perhaps those around him have discovered his secret and are covertly trying to defraud him of his gold preys so keenly upon his mind that he seizes his treasure and hastens to the temple of Fides, where he hides it. Feeling a presentiment of impending misfortune, he returns to the temple and removes the gold to a wood, where he conceals it. Strobilus, a servant of Lyconides, observing the strange conduct of Euclio, follows him, finds the treasure, and runs with it to his master. Lyconides who has heard of the contemplated marriage of his uncle to Phaedra, goes to Euclio to confess the wrong he has done to Phaedra and to beg her in marriage for himself. Upon his appearance Euclio, who has only just discovered the theft of the treasure, is beside himself with alarm, distractedly running here and there in terror and anguish, calling for his gold, and invoking the aid of all in recovering his loss. Lyconides, ignorant of the real cause, believes the outcry is due to the discovery that Phaedra has been betrayed. Without reflecting, he admits that he is culpable, and Euclio interprets this confession of guilt as referring to the gold. The complications that ensue are many, but finally all is explained, and the gold that Strobilus brings to Lyconides is restored to Euclio. That is as far as the play takes us, for the end is missing, but it is not difficult to construct the dénouement. Without doubt, Megadorus renounces his claims to Phaedra in favor of Lyconides, and Euclio, to whom the treasure has been returned, realizing that true happiness does not consist in great wealth, probably shares the treasure with his daughter and her husband.

Such similarity as there is between this Latin play and *El castigo de la miseria* is only discernible in the delineation of the characters of Euclio and D. Marcos. Otherwise the plays are far apart. The incidents are totally dissimilar, and the other characters have nothing in common. Even as to the portrayal of character the two misers are decidedly different. Plautus did not attempt to depict typical avarice. Rather did he try to show the torments of unhappiness and anxiety through which a man passes who has been very poor and then suddenly is overwhelmed by great wealth. Avarice with Euclio was not a vice. It was a trait probably possessed in embryo and not developed until he found the treasure. He lived frugally because he had to do so. He was poor and had a daughter to support; it behooved him to be careful. The discovery of the gold came upon him suddenly; he had no time to reflect, and, unaccustomed to the idea of wealth, he lost his head and acted like a man demented. Previously, Euclio had been resigned to his poverty; he gave no indication of an insatiable desire to accumulate gain, to win for himself position in society. On the other hand, D. Marcos, also poor and needy from his youth, yet of good birth and always a gentleman, was anxious to advance in the world in which he moved. Then as now, money was the " open sesame," and, quick to appreciate this, he practised the small and rigid economies so common and yet so ridiculous in the eyes of the seventeenth century and so pathetic in the present age of gentle humanity. There was nothing dishonorable in his poverty nor in the accumulating of his small fortune. Indeed we are told that he was of excellent habits and held in good repute. By the sweat of his brow, and with personal discomfort, he slowly but steadily gathered together his six thousand ducats. What wonder they were dear to his heart! Necessity, the pinch of poverty, and the honor of the Spanish gentleman, had forced D. Marcos to become niggardly in his habits of living. It is not until he allows his covetousness to influence him in the choice of a wife that he can indeed be called avaricious and a miser in the veritable sense of those words. In the *novela* retribution accomplishes its ends much more effectively than in the drama, for the results are more disastrous.

It is not surprising that Doña María took the subject of avarice for her most interesting novel, nor that she developed it so ingeniously and so successfully, since a familiar figure of her period was the poor but proud *hidalgo* who presented a brave front to society, clinging pathetically to the vestiges of grandeur, yearning for the past splendors of the time when Spain led the world in the glory of her wealth and her achievements. It was a type characteristically Spanish and a natural development of the political, social and economic status of the country. Because he was proud and because he longed to live as a gentleman D. Marcos was incited to economize in order that in time he might fill a position worthy of his ambitions; but as in the case of everything else that is carried to extremes, he succumbed to the pernicious habit, and later allowed it to dominate his life. Doña María may have been familiar with the *Aulularia,* but she did not have to depend upon any foreign source for her inspiration. There were living examples of niggardliness all around her, and in no other place was this more the case than in Madrid. She may have been influenced by Cervantes but she did not have to rely on his portrayal as a model to follow. Her own inventive genius was able to draw from the living examples around her. It was a subject often used by contemporary Spanish writers for the purpose of ridicule. Rather was it more natural for foreign writers seeking such material, to borrow inspiration from Spanish models. Doña María de Zayas has often been cited as influencing *l'Avare* of Molière.[23]  An analysis of Molière's play, however, leaves no doubt as to the fact that the main ideas are taken—as intimated above—from the *Aulularia* of Plautus, but so well is the subject handled, and so original is the development of the characters and the plot, together with the addition of natural wit, that the debt of Molière to Plautus is swallowed up in the superiority of the French production over the Latin play. That Molière was able to read Spanish and was well acquainted with the drama of the peninsula is evident from the fact that in his library were many Spanish plays and that his work shows at times Spanish sources.[24] He was quite frank himself in confessing that he was not over-discriminating in the choice of subjects but made use of whatever he found that suited his purpose. Without doubt he knew the novels of Doña María de Zayas, which not only were popular among her own people, but soon found their way into France. However that may be, Molière has drawn a miser totally different from the hero of the Spanish tale, who has an air of reality about him in his exaggerated sense of economy. Harpagon belongs to a

[23] *Tesoro de Nov. Esp. Ant. y Mod.:* Eugenio de Ochoa. *Molière et le théâtre espagnol:* E. Martinenche. *Molière et l'Espagne:* Guillaume Huszár. Paris, 1907.

[24] *Molière et le théâtre espagnol:* E. Martinenche.

type in which avarice is made an essential characteristic of his nature. He makes a business of being miserly. He has been rich for a long time, has a fine establishment, rich furnishings, good horses for his pleasure and all the appurtenances pertaining to a man of his position, yet with it all he is very close. Poor D. Marcos, born in poverty, has saved for years, and in his saving has been hard on nobody but himself. Harpagon makes his children unhappy because he refuses to provide for them as a man with his means should. He is miserly with his money, not because he wishes to hoard it, rather because he is anxious to increase it through business. He is simply and purely selfish, and his mania makes him appear repellent to us. D. Marcos, with all his faults, is pathetically human. He lacks the sharp astuteness of Harpagon who lends money at exorbitant rates of interest, and seeks to enrich himself at the sacrifice of others. There is no malice in his make-up. He has a child-like trust and confidence in human nature. What he has saved has not been acquired through fraud or misrepresentation. He is essentially honest and not underhanded in any way. Even before marrying Doña Isidora he is quite frank with her concerning his economical proclivities and proposes a plan whereby they may live with little expenditure, saving so that the children they may have may be handsomely provided for. He guards his money carefully, but not frantically as does Harpagon, nor is he secretive about the fact that he has means. Harpagon is afraid he will be thought wealthy and then robbed. D. Marcos by nature is not suspicious.

An interesting character found in both the Spanish and French play is the professional matchmaker, a typical figure of the century, who arranges the match between Harpagon and Mariane as well as that between D. Marcos and Doña Isidora.

The idea of the enumeration of petty savings practised by the miser is found in both the Latin and French plays and in the Spanish tale, although all three are quite different in substance.

In *El castigo de la miseria* we have the intervention of magic, which is not an unnatural proceeding in the fiction and drama of the period.[25] Hardly could Molière have introduced this element

---

[25] *Cf. Coloquio de los perros*, by Cervantes.

into his play, for Harpagon was of too keen and sly a nature to have allowed himself to be so imposed upon. This is an essential difference in the character of the two misers, and for this reason D. Marcos presents an appealing and pitiful figure that produces an effect more tragical than ridiculous.

Emilia Pardo Bazán speaks highly of this novel by Doña María and takes umbrage at the statement made by Navarrete in contradiction of the opinion submitted by Llorente that Doña María de Zayas might well have written the *Gil Blas* and the *Bachiller de Salamanca.*[26] Navarrete does not consider her capable of producing anything as good of its kind. He says that she lacks the necessary observation and intimate knowledge of life which only a man can acquire. Emilia Pardo Bazán feels sure that for the author of *El castigo de la miseria* to compose the *Bachiller de Salamanca* would not have been too arduous a task. She even goes farther and gives her opinion that some of the *Novelas amorosas* will bear favorable comparison with the short stories of Cervantes.[27]

In spite of his adverse criticism concerning her genius, Navarrete, as well as Ochoa, consider this her best production.[28] Perhaps for the reason that it was so good, and original in its ideas, Juan de la Hoz Mota,[29] recognizing its merit, appropriated the plot, dramatized it, and evolved a play[30] which ranks as one of

[26] *Observaciones críticas sobre el Romance de Gil Blas de Santillane,* por Juan Antonio Llorente. Madrid, 1822. Gives a list of thirty-seven who may have been the creators of the original of *Gil Blas* from which the story was taken. Doña María stands fourteenth on the list. "Doña María de Zayas y Sotomayor, natural de Madrid, escribió en 1647 dos tomos de novelas, que suponen en su autora capacidad de componer el *Bachiller* y el *Gil Blas,* si se hubiese dedicado a historias fabulosas mas largas y mas encadenadas que una novela."

[27] " . . . y es de advertir que algunas de las novelas cortas de doña María de Zayas pueden sostener sin desdoro la comparación con otras del manco insigne. Esto no significa que doña María de Zayas fuese capaz de concebir el *Quijote. Quijote* hay uno, uno nada más. Para la autora de *El Castigo de la miseria,* no sería impresa tan ardua escribir el *Bachiller de Salamanca ó La pícara Justina.*" Introduction to *Las Novelas de Doña María de Zayas:* Bibl. de la Mujer; dirigida por Emilia Pardo Bazán.

[28] *Tesoro de Nov. Esp. Ant. y Mod.; Nov. post. á Cervantes:* Navarrete. Bibl. de Aut. Esp.

[29] Born 1620, Madrid.

[30] *El Castigo de la Miseria.*

the best plays of "el teatro antiguo," and whatever fame has survived him is due to this play.[31] He wrote several others but they have been eclipsed by this one, and have fallen into oblivion.[32] It seems at times to have been a question as to whether Juan de la Hoz drew from María de Zayas or vice versa.[33] There can be no doubt as to this if due account is taken of the dates of publication of both works and the date of birth of the two authors. There has even been doubt expressed as to whether the *novela* was the only source for the play. A careful examination of both short story and play will resolve all uncertainties, and establish the fact that Juan de la Hoz could hardly have followed any other model. The general outline is the same, as well as the succession of events and the principal characters. Its merit surely does not rest on its originality, but rather on the happy treatment the author has given the subject in his dramatization. It belongs to the class called *comedias de figurón,* featuring some ridiculous character—a caricature, as it were. Ticknor says it is "one of the best specimens of character drawing on the Spanish stage, and may, in many respects, bear a comparison with the *Aulularia* of Plautus and the *Avare* of Molière."

La Hoz has kept the same names for his principal characters— D. Marcos, Doña Isidora and D. Agustín, but he has added more comedy in the figure of Chinchilla, servant to Agustín and to Doña Isidora, who takes the part of the "gracioso" of the Spanish comedy, and is not found in the story. Another character whose rôle is made more important is D. Marcos' personal servant, a Galician, who furnishes much humor in his peculiarities of speech and the account of his master's mode of living. In the play, it is made very clear that Doña Isidora originates the scheme for deception, and with the consent of Agustín, a student of Salamanca

---

[31] Sismonde de' Sismondi, vol. ii, p. 346; *Nov. post. a Cervantes; Manuel de Literatura:* por Antonio Gil de Zárate. Paris, 1865.

[32] *Principios Generales de Lit. é Hist. de la Lit. española:* por Manuel de la Revilla y Pedro Alcántara García. Madrid 1884. *Manuel de literatura:* por Antonio Gil de Zárate. Paris 1865.

[33] *Colección del Teatro Español:* por García de la Huerta.

[33a] Huerta supposes that it was taken from the novel by Cervantes entitled *El casamiento engañoso.*

with whom she has been intimate, prepares to find a husband for herself. They go to Madrid, hire a house, furnish it richly, and give every appearance of wealth. D. Agustín poses as a nephew of Doña Isidora, who passes as a widow. Once the scheme is formulated, Agustín takes entire charge and Doña Isidora drops into the background. Nothing is told us of the personal appearance of the lady, although in the story this forms a special point of interest. The scene once set, Doña Isidora begins to receive visitors, among them the owner of the house, a certain D. Alonso, who is at once interested in his charming tenant. While paying his call, a noise is heard outside as of someone being persecuted. A servant reports that a horrible spectre of a man is chasing an unfortunate "gallego." At that moment he enters, to escape from his pursuer and in answer to questions describes his master as D. Marcos. Thereupon D. Alonso explains to the company just the kind of man D. Marcos is, qualifying him as the stingiest person in Madrid, "the first to weaken water" (Él inventó aguar el agua), yet one who through his niggardliness has accumulated a fairly large sum of money. The description of D. Marcos given in the play is almost identical with that in the story. Shortly afterwards, Agustín, who thinks D. Marcos just the person to fit into his plans, manages with the aid of the professional matchmaker to interest D. Marcos in the widow who is reputed wealthy. In the *novela,* he is not portrayed in such mercenary guise, for, although interested principally in the wealth he may acquire, yet in his simplicity he is also attracted by the lady.

"Admiróle sobre todo el agrado y discreción de doña Isidora, que parecia la misma gracia, tanto en donaire como en amores, y fueron tantas y tan bien dichas las razones que dijo á don Marcos, que no solo le agradó, mas le enamoró, mostrando en sus agradecimientos el alma que la tenía el buen señor bien sencilla y sin doblez."

This cannot be said of the D. Marcos of the play, whose one thought was of the fortune his wife would bring him, with never a tender sentiment in respect to the lady. On the other hand, Doña María represents Doña Isidora as far more heartless than the same figure in the *comedia;* she is devoid of all kindliness, is hard to the last extremity, and finally does she not make off with all her husband's property, in company with Agustín? Could there be a greater adventuress? But, in the play, when D. Marcos discovers the trick played upon him and asks

"¿ Y me he de quedar casado?"

does not Doña Isidora answer,

> "Eso hasta que yo muera,
> Pues mi amor urdió este engaño,
> Para haceros mi marido."

As in the story, D. Marcos is entertained before his marriage at the home of Doña Isidora in a most elegant manner, and he fully enjoys the delicate food, the gay company, the songs and dances. After his marriage comes the sad awakening, as we already know it. Agustín, who has renewed a love affair with a former sweetheart is anxious to elope, and in order to facilitate his plan persuades Chinchilla to steal the gold which is kept in a chest and which D. Marcos with much care has moved to his bride's home. It consists of six thousand ducats—the same amount as is given in the story. It is interesting to note that Agustín intends to pay back the money as soon as his bride shall receive her dowry. This makes him out a far more respectable figure than in the story. He also has every intention of marrying his sweetheart. In the story, there is no mention of marriage. In fact, after reaching Italy, Inés plies the trade of courtesan to support herself and Agustín.

With the loss of the gold there follows the scene at the magician's with all the attendant circumstances.[34] When D. Marcos cries out in fright, people rush in, among them the personnages involved in the plot. There follow explanations and recriminations but finally all are satisfied with the outcome except D. Marcos who has to make the best of a bad bargain. Unlike the story, his money is returned to him intact, and in this ending it seems that poetic justice fails and that the moral is weak for the perpetrators of the fraud are successful in their machinations and are in no way

[34] Ticknor was mistaken in part when he made the following statement: " The first of these scenes is taken in a good degree, from the *Novelas,* ed. 1637, p. 86; but the scene with the astrologer is wholly the poet's own, and parts of it are worthy of Ben Jonson."

punished for their misdeeds. The question might almost arise as to which are the wrongdoers. As Ticknor says it is " a strange perversion of the original story, for which it is not easy to give a good reason."

The criticism has been made that the last or third act is superfluous as the action according to dramatic rules ends with the second act, but the third act is full of humor and life and does not detract from the interest; rather, does it add to it.[35] La Hoz did the work well, and added a noteworthy contribution to the drama of his country by presenting one of the few plays of this period in which character-drawing was the important feature. At this time little attention was given to development of this sort; instead, the interest concentrated in the events, rapid movement of the action and the unraveling of the plot. There was little reasoning; passion ruled all, and intrigue within intrigue held one in suspense.

The influence of this drama spread into France where an interest in things Spanish held sway at this time. Philarète Chasles writes most emphatically of this period when France surrendered to an interest that included even the Spanish dictionary.[36] Spanish words as well as customs and literature penetrated into France.

"Il n'y avait plus de France française; l'Espagne débordait. On se mit à prendre du chocolat à l'espagnole, à jouer au hoc comme les Espagnols; on donna des *fiestas* sur l'eau, à leur exemple. Mille expressions castillanes nous sont restées. . . . Les femmes prennent la mantille; Amadis fait fureur; le gout des aventures romanesques charme le peuple le plus raisonnable de la terre."
and again farther on, in speaking of the literary influence,

"L'Espagne s'admire, et ses voisins la copient; les oeuvres créées par elle servent d'enseignement à tous. En France, ces germes sont féconds; Scarron leur emprunte les grossières trames d'une intrigue embrouillée et facétie populaire des Picaros; d'Urfé amuse les femmes en imitant les fantaisies bergeresque, etc."

So it was not strange that popular novels and plays from Spain should find their way into France, and that new and unusual themes should be seized upon by French authors, seeking variety, and transmitted to the public. Scarron was one of these to avail himself of

---

[35] Ticknor; Zárate.

[36] *Études sur l'Espagne, et sur les influences de la littérature espagnole en France et en Italie.*

some of the most piquantes Spanish compositions. He did not improve upon them, nor did he add anything original. He simply translated them into his own tongue, but he made the grave mistake of not making this clear to the public, publishing them without the slightest mention of their respective authors. The translations appeared apparently as his own original work. Unfortunately for him, D'Ouville who had spent seven years in Spain in the service of the Count of Dognon and had the chance to become familiar with the Spanish productions, shortly after the translations by Scarron appeared, published a collection of Spanish tales (1656), admittedly translations, and in his preface twitted Scarron with the intent to deceive. Thereupon resulted a bitter quarrel which was continued even after D'Ouville's death between Scarron and D'Ouville's brother, Boisrobert, who carried on his work. In the *Nouvelles-tragi-comiques* of Scarron are several novels by Doña María de Zayas, but of particular interest at this point is the one entitled *Châtiment de l'Avarice* which is a fairly good translation of the novela *El castigo de la miseria*. In this he probably saw in its realism and caricature the germs of burlesque—that type of humor later developed by him, and was tempted to include it in his work. When pressed by his enemies, he admitted the truth about the translations but claimed that he had improved upon them and that the originals were written in extremely poor Spanish! Paul Morillot in his book *Scarron, Étude Biographique et Littéraire,* (Paris, 1888), can see no reason why Scarron should be blamed in any way nor that he suffered from the exposure. He adds that his work was far superior to either D'Ouville's or María de Zayas' and that he added so much from his own inventive genius that he saved the work of Doña María de Zayas from oblivion![37] "N'est-ce pas le cas de dire que la façon a peut-être mieux valu que l'étoffe?" A comparison of the two works fails to reveal any basis for such reasoning. All credit is due to Doña María for a piece of work remarkable for its originality, freshness of interest and elegance of expression. It cannot be reasonably maintained that Scarron or anyone else has either improved upon it, or has added to its intrinsic merits.

[37] I have been unable to consult the translation by D'Ouville.

## VITA

The writer was born in New Bedford, Massachusetts, and received her preliminary education in the schools of that city. From 1908 to 1912 she attended Smith College, from which she was graduated with the degree of A.B. After pursuing graduate studies at Columbia University during the regular session of 1913–1914 she received the degree of A.M. from Columbia University. From 1914 to 1919, while acting as head of the Department of Spanish in the High School of Hackensack, New Jersey, she continued graduate studies at Columbia. The year 1920–1921, spent in California, gave opportunity for research at the Universities of California and Southern California. The academic year 1921–1922 was devoted to further study and to the completion of the present dissertation.

Bei Fragen zur Produktsicherheit wenden Sie sich bitte an:
If you have any questions regarding product safety,
please contact:

Walter de Gruyter GmbH
Genthiner Straße 13
10785 Berlin
productsafety@degruyterbrill.com